BLACKFEET INDIANS

BLACKFEET INDIANS

PICTURES BY WINOLD REISS

STORY BY FRANK B LINDERMAN

GRAMERCY BOOKS
NEW YORK • AVENEL

This 1995 edition is published by Gramercy Books,
distributed by Random House Value Publishing, Inc.,
40 Engelhard Avenue,
Avenel, New Jersey 07001

Random House
New York • Toronto • London • Sydney • Auckland

Printed and bound in the United States of America

Library of Congress Cataloging–in–Publication Data

Linderman, Frank Bird.
    Blackfeet Indians / Frank Linderman ; illustrated by Winold Reiss.
        p. cm.
    ISBN 0-517-14807-2
    1. Siksika Indians. 2. Indians of North America—Great Plains.
I. Title.
E99 . S54L5 1995
978 ' . 004973—dc20   95-18001
                        10 9 8 7 6 5 4 3 2 1

DEDICATED TO THE BLACKFEET
HEROIC INDIANS OF THE PLAINS
WHOSE NOBLE SPIRIT WILL LIVE
AS AN INSPIRATION TO ALL WHO
MEET THEM WITH AN OPEN HEART

THE DRUMMERS — SURE CHIEF, BUFFALO BODY AND HEAVY BREAST. THE BLACKFEET ARE A MUSICAL PEOPLE AND LOVE TO DRUM AND SING ON ALL OCCASIONS.

FOREWORD

This book really needs no introduction. It is a book of beauty that is sadness; of courage that inspires; of duplicity that makes a white man's conscience squirm. It is a book of loneliness, the awful loneliness that fills the world from earth to sky, when a soul has lost its gods, its faith, its bearings.

It was created in response to calls from people, who through their visits to Glacier National Park, became interested in the Blackfeet Indians of the adjoining reservation and were anxious to learn something of their life before the reservation hemmed them in and made them farmer-ranchers; and, also, in response to calls from persons, who having seen isolated examples of Winold Reiss's paintings of the Blackfeet, wanted an authentic collection of his work. Having access to the colorful portraits that Mr. Reiss has made among the Bloods and Piegans, the Great Northern Railway asked Frank Bird Linderman, author of INDIAN WHY STORIES, THE AMERICAN, *and other books about the plains Indians, to write the story of the Blackfeet as he learned it by a lifetime of spoken and sign-language inquiry among the Old Ones of the tribe; the Old Ones who remember the legends and records of their nomadic forbears.*

These pages will be turned over and over again. For the pictures offer limitless detail, unnumbered motifs; they are filled with color and contrast; with primitive design and magnificent craftsmanship. Mr. Linderman's story offers insight, information, interpretation. It is as simple as the Psalms. Beaverlike it bites through bark to the solid tissue of truth. It will be read again and again for the understanding it gives, for the swift flow of its thought...from the years of Blackfeet content down through the turbulent days of fur traders and skin hunters, to the proud and stoic remnants of a once great tribe that we moderns meet during the golden months of summer.

And, finally, this volume will suggest some strange thoughts to us who talk about our modern standards of living...who turn on heat and light and music...who project our voices through the air and over slender wires...who cheat the heat of summer and the cold of winter...who travel in luxury across the plains where not so long ago the Blackfeet roamed on foot or horseback—the primitive Blackfeet, happy with few possessions and fewer comforts, yet doomed to disillusion from the day the civilized white man first appeared on their horizon.

W. M.

THE PEMMICAN MAKERS — PECUN-
NIE WOMEN SITTING IN THEIR
TEPEE MIXING DRIED SERVICE
BERRIES AND MEAT TO MAKE
PEMMICAN.

OUT OF THE NORTH

By FRANK B. LINDERMAN

BLACKFEET! No tribal name appears oftener in the history of the Northwestern plains; no other is so indelibly written into the meager records of the early fur-trade of the upper Missouri river, and none ever inspired more dread in white plainsmen. Hell-gate* was not so named because the water there was fiercely wild, or the mountain trail difficult, but because the way led from tranquillity to trouble, to the lands of the hostile Blackfeet.

The three tribes of the Blackfeet nation, the Pecunnies (Piegans), Bloods, and Blackfeet, are one people. They speak a common language, and practice the same customs. Long ago, probably more than two hundred years, the Blackfeet were a timber people inhabiting the forests near Lesser Slave lake. Incessant war forced upon them by the powerful Chippewas (Ojibwas) pushed them steadily southward until they reached the wide plains bordering the Rocky mountains in what is now Montana. Here they found vast herds of fat buffalo, elk, and antelope, an exhaustless abundance they had never known; and here, after driving the Snakes, and probably the Flatheads, Kootenais, and Nez Perces, from the bountiful grass-lands to the narrow valleys west of the Rockies, the three tribes of Blackfeet settled down to become plainsmen. Nobody can tell their numbers when they came out of the north. Old Pecunnie warriors have told me that their tribe once counted 750 lodges, probably less than 4000 people; and we know that, of the three tribes of the Blackfeet nation, the Pecunnie was the most numerous.

All this happened before the Blackfeet had horses. Dogs had always transported their goods. Now, to steal horses, their raiding parties ranged over the endless grass-lands far toward the south, old warriors say even into the Spanish possessions. Often these raiders were absent for two years; and nearly always they were successful. Their pony-bands grew until men measured their wealth in horses. Meat, their principal food, was easily obtained; and yet these people did not permit life to drag, or become stale. War and horse-stealing were their never-ending games; and besides furnishing necessary excitement and adventure they kept every man in constant training, since a successful raid was certain to bring attempts at reprisal. To be mentioned by his tribesmen as a great warrior, or a cunning horse-thief, was the highest ambition of a plains Indian; and the Blackfeet were master-hands at both these

---

*Near Missoula, Montana. Gateway through the Rockies to the plains.

hazardous hobbies. When finally they obtained fire-arms they became the scourge of the Northwestern plains, claiming all the country lying north of the Yellowstone river to the Saskatchewan. In stature they average taller than the men of neighboring tribes, having thin, shapely noses, and intelligent faces. Like the other tribesmen of the great grass-lands they were naturally a deeply religious people; and like all the plains Indians they were naturally jolly, loving jest and laughter when not in the presence of strangers.

Even though the Blackfeet may have brought their social customs from the northern forests, they did not differ greatly from those of the other plains people. Each of the three tribes was subdivided into clans, or gentes of blood kin in the male line, there being in the Blackfeet nation perhaps fifty such clans known as Black-Elks, Lone-Fighters, Fat-Roasters, White-Breasts, etc. A man was not permitted by tribal law to marry a woman who belonged to his own clan; and the children of any union belonged always to their mother's clan. Young women were closely guarded. There was little courting. Marriages were arranged by parents, with the consent of near relations. And yet, when possible, the desires of young people were given consideration. Nevertheless the father of a young woman finally decided the question of marriage for his daughter; and there were many things which a father must consider in making this decision. He must think of the young man's breeding, prestige, and his power to provide properly for a family. He must not forget that upon giving his daughter in marriage he automatically made all her younger sisters the potential wives of her husband, and that even though his son-in-law might never demand any of them they could not be otherwise disposed of without the son-in-law's consent. Moreover he must remember that if his son-in-law should die all his wives would become the potential wives of his son-in-law's oldest brother. These matters often led fathers to forbid their daughters marrying the young men of their choice; and then sometimes the unhappy young women hanged themselves. However, when an agreement was reached the young woman's mother outfitted her with pretty clothes, besides making a new buffalo-skin lodge for the young couple. During all these preparations, requiring weeks, accompanied by her mother or a girl friend, the bride-to-be, under the eyes of the village, each day carried prepared food to the lodge of her future husband. When at last the wedding-lodge had been pitched in the center of the encampment, the bride's mother accompanied her daughter to her new home, helped her arrange her household, and then left her there. Her father now tied a dower of several horses, all he could afford, to his daughter's lodge, sometimes, to show his respect for his future son-in-law, even adding his own war-shield and most prized weapons. The young man, seeing that all was in readiness, now entered the wedding-lodge, seating himself at its "head." And from that minute he was forever forbidden to speak to his mother-in-law, or to her sisters; and he could not in propriety pronounce their names. By the same tribal law his mother-in-law and her sisters were forbidden to speak to *him*, or *of* him, by name. If a woman suddenly met her son-in-law in the village she either turned aside or in passing covered her face with her robe. This is the reason for the signs, *ashamed woman*, often made by old plains Indians in referring to a man's mother-in-law.

Blackfeet children were named *only as individuals*. Family, or sur-names, were not used, so that there was seldom anything in a person's name that even remotely suggested ancestry. Children were often named by their grandparents, or other aged relations, dreams usually suggesting the names chosen. Sometimes the one commissioned for the office named a baby for the first thing seen on the morning after receiving the commission, birds and animals supplying most of such names. However, a grown man might change his own name every time he *counted coup** in battle, or once each year if he desired. Oldtime Blackfeet would seldom speak their names aloud, believing that to do so might bring misfortune.

Beyond the gift of horses or goods to the woman's father there was no ceremony, and little formality, in a plural marriage. A man's first wife was known as *His-Sits-Beside-Him-Woman*. Her place was near the "head" of the lodge on her husband's right. She superintended the lodge, and the work of the other wives, who were often her sisters; and she possessed special privileges. She might, at times, take part in the conversation of her husband and his guests, and she might, during informal meetings, even smoke the pipe when it was passed in her lodge. The other wives sat near the door, which is always directly opposite the "head" of the lodge.

Smoking was a sacred ceremony. Old plains Indians sealed oaths and agreements with the pipe. In smoking, the host or master of ceremonies, filled and lighted the stone pipe, offering its stem first to the sun (the father) and then to the earth (the mother) before smoking, himself. Next he passed the pipe to the guest on his *left*, "as the sun travels." After smoking, usually taking three deep draughts, this guest handed the pipe to the man on *his* left, the pipe's stem being kept pointed at the lodge-wall in its movements. And the pipe must not be handed across the doorway. When the man nearest the door on the host's left hand had smoked, the pipe must go back to the "head" of the lodge where the host passed it to the guest on his *right*, the pipe going, unsmoked to the guest nearest the door on that side. When this guest had smoked he passed the pipe to the guest on his *left*, so that the pipe again began to move "as the sun travels." If the pipe needed refilling it was

---

* Note: The term *coup*, meaning a blow, is attributable to the early French voyageur.

handed back to the host who replenished it, the guests passing it along, unsmoked, to the man who had discovered its emptiness. Nobody might properly pass between smokers and the lodge-fire.

Hereditary leadership was unknown. Men became chiefs by their prowess in war; and because he must ever be generous, a chief was usually a poor man. With the Blackfeet, as with the other Indians of the Northwestern plains, a chieftainship had to be maintained by constant demonstration of personal ability. It might easily be lost in a single day, since these independent tribesmen were free to choose their leaders, and were quick to desert a weak or cowardly character. This independence was instilled in the children of the plains people. They were never whipped, or severely punished. The boys were constantly lectured by the old men of the tribes, exhorted to strive for renown as warriors, and to die honorably in battle before old age came to them. The names of tribal heroes were forever upon the tongues of these teachers; and everywhere cowardice was bitterly condemned. A coward was forbidden to marry, and he must at all times wear women's clothing.

The girls were taught by their mothers and grandmothers to look seriously upon life, to shun the frivolous, and to avoid giggling. With the Blackfeet, women "gave" the sun-dances, the most sacred of their religious ceremonies; and because the "givers" of these sun-dances must have lived exemplary lives to have dared offer dances to the sun, they were forever afterward highly honored by both the men and women of the tribe. "Look, my daughter," a woman would say, "there goes Two-Stars. She is *The-Sits-Beside-Him-Woman* of White-Wolf. Two summers ago she gave a sun-dance, and she yet lives. If you try to be like her you may some day give a sun-dance, yourself." Girls were warned by their mothers against infidelity to their husbands, since adultery cost a married woman her nose, or ears; for a second offense she was killed by her brothers, or first cousins, upon formal complaint by her husband. By tribal law murder was punished by death, or by stripping the murderer of all property for the benefit of the dead man's family, the latter choosing the penalty. Proven treachery, which amounted to treason, was also punished by death; and a thief was compelled to return the stolen goods to their rightful owner.

The lodges, or tepees, of the plains Indians were the most comfortable transportable shelters ever devised by man. They were made of grained, and partially dressed, buffalo cow skins, from fourteen to twenty-four skins being required for a lodge. Indian women could easily pitch or strike a lodge within a few minutes. In cold weather the lodges were made comfortable, besides being brightened interiorly, by handsomely decorated linings which reached well above the heads of seated occupants, thus protecting them from draughts. From fourteen to twenty-six slender poles were required for each lodge, their length depending upon the height of the lodge. New sets of poles were usually cut each year, since dragging them over the plains in following the buffalo herds wore them out in a season. Lodges were often decorated with picture-stories of *medicine-dreams*, scalps, and buffalo-tails. In the village each clan, and each individual lodge, had its rightful position, the lodges of clan chieftains being pitched in a small circle within the village-circle, each always occupying its hereditary post.

Indians of the plains respect dignity and love formality. Conventional decorum, easy and masterful, was always evident in the lodges of old plains warriors. From the host's place at the "head" of a lodge his sons sat at his left, according to age; his wives, and their visiting women friends, on his right. A male guest, upon entering a lodge, turned to his right, around the lodge-fire, and was promptly assigned a seat on the host's left, according to his rank as a warrior. If a visitor had a message he stood while delivering it; and he was never interrupted for any reason until he had finished speaking, and had so declared. Once within a lodge even an enemy might speak as he chose without interference or heckling. After leaving the village he must look out for himself, however.

Basketry and the making of pottery were unknown to the Blackfeet. Their weapons, clothing, and robes received most of their artistic attention, the three-pronged design representing the three tribes of the nation being commonly used. Most of their bows were made of ash, or the wood of the chokecherry, their arrows being made of the shoots of service-berry bushes. Their shields were of rawhide taken from the necks of old buffalo-bulls. They would turn an arrow, and are said to have often turned bullets fired from old-fashioned rifles. The oldtime pipes of the Blackfeet were made of black, or greenish, stone, "straight" pipes sometimes being used in ceremonials.

The men wore shirts, breech-clouts, leggings, and moccasins, the latter soled with rawhide. In summer they wore no head-gear unless attending a ceremonial. In winter the men often wore caps made from the skins of animals or water-fowl. Eagle feathers were often worn by the men, beautiful war-bonnets being made with them. The women wore gowns of dressed deer, antelope, or mountain-sheep, skins that reached nearly to their ankles; and they also wore leggings, moccasins, and decorated belts carrying knives in painted scabbards.

The men were thorough sportsmen, loving horse-racing, foot-racing, and gambling. They were graceful winners, and good losers in games of chance. And they were firm believers in luck, and in the *medicine* conferred in dreams. Men often starved, and even tortured themselves, in preparation for desired *medicine-dreams*. Then, weakened both physically and mentally by enervating sweat-baths and fatigue, they slipped away alone to some dangerous spot, usually a high mountain-peak, a sheer cliff, or a well-worn buffalo-trail that might be traveled at any hour by a vast herd of buffalo; and here, without food, or water, they spent four days and nights (if necessary) trying to dream, appealing to invisible "helpers," crying aloud to the winds until utter exhaustion brought them sleep, or unconsciousness—and perhaps a *medicine-dream*. If lucky, some animal or bird appeared to the dreamer, offering counsel and help, nearly always prescribing rules which if followed would lead the dreamer to success in war. Thereafter the bird or animal appearing in the *medicine-dream* was the dreamer's *medicine*. He believed that all the power, the cunning, and the instinctive wisdom, possessed by the appearing bird or animal would forever afterward be his own in time of need. And always thereafter the dreamer carried with him some part of such bird or animal. It was his lucky-piece, a talisman, and he would undertake nothing without it upon his person.

In each of the three tribes of Blackfeet there were several societies, some of them being secret organizations. Most of them were military in character, some of them originally having police power over villages; and at least one of them was composed of boys who were not yet old enough to go to war. The Horn society of the Bloods, and the Kit-Foxes of the Pecunnies, seem to have been much the same society; and it may have been the most honorable and exclusive. The women of the Pecunnie also had a society which is said to have been secret. It was evidently not unlike the Horns in standing, since none but women of middle-age whose lives were known to have been upright were eligible to membership. This society selected its members, electing them before solicitation, one dissenting vote excluding a proposed woman.

Like all Indians of the plains, the Blackfeet formerly placed deep faith in the *medicine-men*, the "wise-ones" of their tribes; and even though these men resorted to intricate ceremonies which fascinated patients and onlookers there is no doubt that they often healed the sick and wounded through this faith alone. They did, however, possess considerable knowledge of the medicinal properties of herbs and roots, and often prescribed them. There was little sickness, since the daily lives of the plains Indians kept them in perfect physical condition. Sunrise saw most of the men and boys in the icy streams, winter and summer alike.

Burial of the dead was usually on platforms lashed to the limbs of trees beyond the reach of wolves. Securely wrapped in buffalo robes, firmly bound with rawhide thongs, the bodies were safe from ravens, crows, and magpies. Weapons and pipes were buried with warriors, root-diggers and cooking utensils with the women. Often a number of horses were killed at the burial of a warrior, so that his spirit might ride in

The Sand Hills, the Heaven of the Blackfeet. In mourning for a son, or other male relative, both men and women scarified themselves, and cut off their hair, the women wailing piteously, sometimes for long periods. The mourning for women was of shorter duration, and not so wild.

The Blackfeet were meat eaters. Meat constituted fully 90% of their daily fare. It was either boiled or roasted, "meat-holes," which operated as fireless-cookers, being sometimes used. Roots and bulbs were also cooked in the ground; and the eggs of water-fowl were often steamed. Berries were eaten fresh; and they were dried for winter use, the latter being used in making the best pemmican, a mixture of dried, lean meat thoroughly pulverized and seasoned with the berries and bone-marrow. Ordinary pemmican was made with dried meat and melted tallow, no berries being used. The Blackfeet did not have salt, and like all the plains tribes dried their meat in the sun, unsalted, packing it away for winter use, the pemmican in buffalo-skin bags.

In the days before the white man came to the plains the Blackfeet were a happy people. An abundance of material for their food, clothing, and sheltering lodges was constantly in sight on every hand. Beyond these necessities their needs were few, so that with a firm belief in the exhaustless bounty of their loved grass-lands these practical folks lived each day for itself. And they knew how to live. Their pride in themselves forbade too much ease, even in their land of plenty. No successful hunter, no tribesman who, with crude weapons, plentifully fed a family, could have been a lazy man, no perfect horseman a weakling. The arms and wrists of men who could send arrows down to their feathers into the bodies of huge buffalo bulls were as powerful as spring steel; and men who loved war for its excitement could not have been weak-hearted. The power of endurance of the plains Indians has always been beyond comprehension by white men. These tribesmen hunted, feasted, gambled, and eagerly made war, young men often faring forth alone over the unmarked plains to *count coup*, so that they might marry the young women of their choice, and be numbered among the tribe's warriors. Killing and scalping an enemy did not entitle them to *count coup*. They must strike an armed enemy with their hands, or with something held in their hands, without otherwise injuring the enemy; or they must capture an enemy's weapons, or be first to strike an enemy who had fallen in battle, etc., the rules for *coup-counting* differing somewhat among the plains tribes. And this *coup-counting* was expected of young men. For centuries, during the long, winter nights on these northern plains, red patriarchs feelingly extolled bravery and fortitude, reciting hero-tales, some of which may have had origin in far lands.* They were a change-less people, a romantically happy people, until the white man came to the plains.

* I once found one of them in a translation from the Sanskrit.

The Blackfeet instinctively opposed the coming of white trappers and traders. Nevertheless the fur companies built forts on the upper Missouri in the heart of the Pecunnie country; and nowhere has the white man stooped so low for gain as in the fur trade of the Northwest; nowhere has he been so reprehensible as in his treatment of the plains Indian. Besides his trade-whisky he brought infectious maladies to a people whose blood was clean. Nobody will ever know half the crimes that were committed by these avaricious traders. The enforced inoculation of a large band of visiting Indians with the virus of smallpox taken from the pustules on the body of a stricken white *engagee* at Fort Union, whose blood was known to be otherwise unclean, is revolting enough, especially when one knows that the step was taken wholly in the interest of the traders who hoped to have the scourge over with before the fall trading began. It is even more revolting when one learns that all the vaccinated Indians perished; and yet this deed is no more fiendish in character than the discharge of a cannon loaded with ounce trade-balls into a crowd of unsuspecting Pecunnies who were visiting at Fort McKenzie, a little below Fort Benton, in the year 1843.

The American Fur Company's steamboat, Trapper, brought smallpox up the river in 1837. This devastating scourge swept through the tribes of the Northwestern plains like a poisoned gale. Nobody knows how many Indians perished, estimates ranging from 60,000 to 200,000 men, women, and children. Perhaps the least of these figures is high. Nevertheless the Mandans alone lost 6000 members, so that when the plague had spent itself the tribe had but 32 warriors left alive. Reaching Fort McKenzie the disease first attacked the inmates, deaths occurring so rapidly that burial was impossible. The dead bodies were thrown into the Missouri river. Within the fort there were 29 deaths, 26 of them being Pecunnie women who had been attached to the fort's *engagees.* Upon the arrival of the disease-laden boat there had been 500 lodges of Blackfeet camped at Fort McKenzie. Now they were gone. During all the time that the smallpox had scourged the fort's company not an Indian appeared on the plains.

In October Alexander Culbertson, the American Fur Company's manager at McKenzie, set out to learn what might have happened to his patrons. He did not have to travel far before reaching a village of 60 Pecunnie lodges standing among the dead bodies of hundreds of men, women and children, and even of horses and dogs. Here, in these horrid surroundings Culbertson found two old women, too feeble to travel, chanting their *death-songs* among the putrid dead. And here, having seen enough, Alexander Culbertson, the trader, turned back to his fort.

In November straggling groups of Blackfeet came to Fort McKenzie to tell their awful story. The disease had not made its appearance among them until the tenth day after leaving the post. Then its ravaging became so terrible that in the ensuing panic young warriors who fell ill stabbed themselves to death rather than have their fine bodies wasted and scarred by the loathsome disease. More than 6000 Blackfeet had perished, they said, more than half their nation. Many other tribes suffered as severely, the Assiniboins losing more than three-quarters of their warriors.

Nevertheless the trade in buffalo robes was that fall and winter greater than ever before at Forts McKenzie and Union, since dead Indians needed no robes. Stripped by thousands from their bodies by surviving tribesmen, these death-robes were traded in at the Company's forts; and then, without the least attempt at disinfection, they were shipped to "the states" where, providentially, no epidemic of smallpox ensued. But the weakened tribes never again regained their numbers. Ever since 1837 these Indians have been failing physically. This is not only because their best blood perished in the plague of that year, but because whole clans having been wiped out, inter-breeding ensued.

During all this time the heavy toll upon the immense herds of buffalo in the Northwest was scarcely noticeable; and now there was an exodus of traders. Having stripped the section of its beaver and land-fur, these avaricious white men began to abandon their trading-posts on the river, and to leave the country to the Indians and hungry wolves.

The Blackfeet, weakened in numbers, and tortured with bitter recollections, had scarcely settled down to their old life when the Seventies brought the professional skin-hunters to the plains. And now, for from 50 cents to $1.50 per head, these white men shot down the buffalo for their robes alone, leaving countless thousands of tons of fat meat to rot where it fell. By the middle Eighties the skin-hunters had finished. The buffalo were gone forever. The wide grass-lands, which for centuries had been so bountiful, were bleak, inhospitable, and bare. Even the elk and antelope had been wiped away. The Blackfeet, and all the Indians of the plains, were hungry now; and even while the Pecunnies searched in vain for the vanished herds, which the old warriors believed had hidden away, more than one-quarter of the tribe starved to death.

Dazed, unable to comprehend the terrible calamity which had overtaken them, clinging doggedly to their belief that the buffalo had hidden, and would soon return to their loved grass-lands, the Pecunnies were slow to rally. If the tardy Government of the United States had not acted the Pecunnies would have perished to a man.

But the Government did act at last; and the work of making wild hunters into gentle farmers in a single generation began. And this work is succeeding. The Pecunnies, and all the Blackfeet, are rapidly becoming self-supporting by raising cattle and crops on the old buffalo range.

LONG BEFORE ANYBODY HAD DREAMED OF GLACIER NATIONAL PARK THE BLACK-FEET SOLD A PORTION OF THEIR MOUNTAINOUS LANDS TO THE GOVERNMENT OF THE UNITED STATES FOR $1,500,000 TO BE PAID IN ANNUAL INSTALLMENTS OF $150,000 FOR TEN YEARS, BEGINNING IN 1887. THIS SALE, MADE SO SOON AFTER THE BUFFALO HAD DISAPPEARED, WAS A BLESSING TO THE TRIBE, SOME OF THE PROCEEDS BEING INVESTED IN CATTLE TO GRAZE ON THE EXTENSIVE LEVEL LANDS WHICH THE IN-DIANS RETAINED. IN 1895-6 THE TRIBE SOLD MORE OF THEIR MOUNTAINS TO THE UNITED STATES GOVERNMENT, AND IN 1910, WHEN GLACIER NATIONAL PARK WAS CREATED, THESE MOUNTAINS BECAME THE MOST ATTRACTIVE SECTION OF THE PARK.

TODAY THERE ARE ABOUT NINE HUNDRED FULL-BLOOD PECUNNIES LIVING ON THEIR LANDS WHICH ADJOIN THIS GREAT NATIONAL PARK. THESE INDIANS YET HAVE THEIR TRIBAL COUNCIL, THEIR DANCES, AND CEREMONIALS, AND EVEN THOUGH THE GOVERNMENT CONTINUES TO SUPERINTEND THEM AND THEIR WORKS, THEY ARE ALL CITIZENS OF THE UNITED STATES.

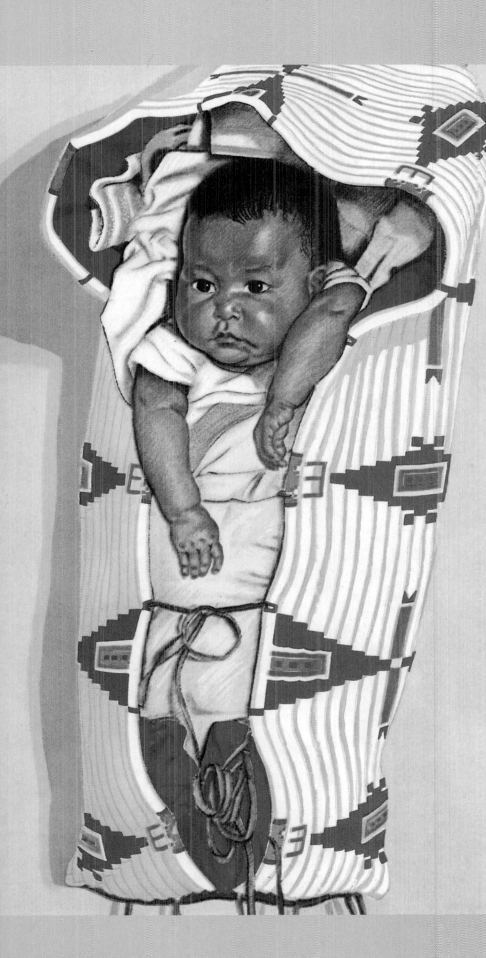

SNOW BIRD — IN CARRIER. THE
BLACKFEET, BEING A NOMADIC
PEOPLE. DEVISED THE CARRIER
AS A SAFE MEANS OF TRANS-
PORTATION FOR THEIR BABIES.
IT WAS CARRIED EITHER ON THE
WOMAN'S BACK OR TIED TO THE
DOG OR HORSE TRAVOIS.

TWO GUNS—SON OF ONE OF THE LAST GREAT PECUNNIE CHIEFTAINS, WHITE CALF, WHO DIED IN WASHINGTON, D. C. IN 1904, WHILE THERE ON A MISSION FOR HIS PEOPLE. PRESIDENT THEODORE ROOSEVELT SENT HIS REMAINS BACK TO THE RESERVATION IN MONTANA WITH A MILITARY ESCORT.

NENAUAKI — A YOUNG WOMAN OF THE BLOOD TRIBE, CONSIDERED BY MR. REISS TO BE ONE OF THE MOST BEAUTIFUL INDIAN WOMEN HE EVER PAINTED.

YELLOW HEAD — ONE OF THE FINEST LOOKING MEN OF THE PECUNNIES OR MONTANA BLACK-FEET. EDUCATED IN A GOVERN-MENT SCHOOL HE SPEAKS ENG-LISH FLUENTLY BUT STILL AD-HERES TO THE CUSTOMS OF HIS FOREFATHERS.

DOUBLE STEEL AND TWO CLT-
TER — THESE WOMEN OF THE
BLOOD TRIBE ARE WELL KNOWN
FOR THEIR BEAD WORK.

SHORT MAN — AN EXPERT IN THE INDIAN SIGN LANGUAGE. HE WON HIGHEST HONORS IN A COMPETITION GIVEN BY THE LATE GENERAL HUGH L. SCOTT, WHO WAS AN AUTHORITY ON THE SIGN LANGUAGE OF THE PLAINS INDIANS.

TWO GUNS — HIS OUTSTANDING
PERSONALITY, COMBINED WITH
RARE ORATORICAL TALENT, SE-
CURED FOR HIM MANY FRIENDS
ON HIS EXTENSIVE TRAVELS.
WITH HIS DEATH IN 1934 THE
UNITED STATES LOST ONE OF
ITS MOST MAJESTIC INDIANS.

JUNIPER BUFFALO BULL AND
LITTLE YOUNG MAN — TWO OF
THE YOUNGER PECUNNIE BRAVES
IN THEIR FESTIVE COSTUMES.
JUNIPER BUFFALO BULL IS WEAR-
ING A MEDICINE NECKLACE OF
BEAR CLAWS.

MORNING GUN — KNOWN AS THE "KINDEST INDIAN" THROUGHOUT MOST OF HIS LIFE, HE STILL LEFT A RECORD OF EXTREME BRAVERY AS A WARRIOR, WHEN HE DIED IN 1934. FULL OF HUMOR AND KINDNESS, A SUCCESSFUL RANCHER IN HIS LATER YEARS, HE WAS AN OUTSTANDING MEMBER OF THE PECUNNIE TRIBE.

SPOPEIA AND MAMEIA — SPOPEIA
AT THE AGE OF 12 ALREADY SHOWS
THE INDIAN'S CREATIVE ABILITY
IN ART. HE HAS MADE MANY ORIG-
INAL DRAWINGS AND PAINTINGS
FULL OF ACTION AND COLOR.

SHOT ON BOTH SIDES — CHIEF OF THE BLOOD INDIANS. IN THE GOVERNING OF HIS TRIBE, HIS DIPLOMACY AND LEADERSHIP HAVE DONE A GREAT DEAL TOWARDS MAKING HIS PEOPLE SELF-SUPPORTING.

LONG TIME PIPE WOMAN — WIFE
OF CHIEF SHOT ON BOTH SIDES.
SHE IS WEARING A BUCKSKIN
DRESS, THE TOP OF WHICH IS
RICHLY BEADED WITH BLACK-
FEET MOTIFS.

EAGLE PLUME — GRANDSON OF
CHIEF SHOT ON BOTH SIDES.

EAGLE CALF—EDUCATED AT CAR-
LISLE UNIVERSITY, HE RETURN-
ED TO THE INDIAN LIFE AND IS
ONE OF THE ABLE INTERPRETERS
OF HIS PEOPLE. HE IS ALSO AN
INDUSTRIOUS RANCHER WITH A
LARGE FAMILY TO CARE FOR.

MANY HORSES, LITTLE ROSE-
BUSH, AND BABY — THREE GEN-
ERATIONS OF PECUNNIES.

MANY MULES—AN OLD WARRIOR
OF THE BLOOD TRIBE. EIGHTY-
TWO YEARS OLD AND ALMOST
BLIND, HE RODE THIRTY MILES
ON HORSEBACK TO HAVE HIS
PORTRAIT PAINTED.

JAMES WHITE CALF — NOT SO
WELL KNOWN OFF THE RESERVA-
TION AS HIS BROTHER, TWO
GUNS, WHO HAD TRAVELED EX-
TENSIVELY, BUT A SUCCESSFUL
FARMER AND A FAMILIAR AND
COLORFUL FIGURE AT ALL PE-
CUNNIE TRIBAL FUNCTIONS.

ONLY CHILD — PECUNNIE GIRL.
SHE IS SITTING AGAINST A BACK-
REST MADE OF THIN WILLOW
STICKS. SUCH BACK-RESTS ARE
USED IN THE BLACKFEET TE-
PEES AND ARE ONE OF THE MANY
ACCESSORIES WHICH MAKE THE
TEPEE ONE OF THE MOST COM-
FORTABLE PLACES TO LIVE IN.

HOME GUN — A QUIET AND SOLEMN MEDICINE MAN OF THE PECUNNIES. POSSESSOR OF THE SACRED "BEAVER BUNDLE" AND OTHER PRECIOUS INDIAN MEDICINES. IN THE POWER OF THESE AND HIS SACRED PIPE HE TRUSTS FOR BENEFITS TO HIS FAMILY, HIS FRIENDS AND HIS PEOPLE.

HEAVY BREAST — ONE OF THE
BEST INTERPRETERS, WHO HAS
HELPED WINOLD REISS MANY A
TIME TO DISCOVER INTERESTING
TYPES FROM REMOTE PARTS OF
THE RESERVATION.

GOOD STRIKER — AN OLD BLOOD WARRIOR. HE WAS PRESENT AT THE LAST FIGHT WITH THE CREES NEAR THE SITE OF LETHBRIDGE, ALBERTA. A LEADER PROUD OF THE TRADITIONS OF HIS PEOPLE.

CUT NOSE WOMAN — WEARING A HUDSON BAY BLANKET FOR WHICH THE INDIANS TRADED BUFFALO ROBES IN THE OLD DAYS. THE SIZE AND WEIGHT OF THESE BLANKETS WERE IN- DICATED BY "POINTS," SIGNI- FYING THEIR TRADE VALUE IN SKINS.

MIKE OKA—A PICTURESQLE
BLOOD TRIBESMAN WHO WAS
PRESENT AS A BOY IN 1877 AT
THE SIGNING OF THE TREATY
OF BLACKFOOT CROSSING BE-
TWEEN THE CANADIAN GOVERN-
MENT AND THE INDIANS. FCR
SOME YEARS HE WAS AN INDIAN
SCOUT WITH THE ROYAL NORTH-
WEST MOUNTED POLICE.

LITTLE PLUME — A PECUNNIE
BRAVE. THE BACKGROUND IS A
GOOD EXAMPLE OF THE INDIAN
PICTURE-WRITING. BY SUCH
DRAWINGS THEY EXPRESSED THE
MOST IMPORTANT EXPLOITS OF
THEIR LIVES.

DOG TAKING GUN — AN EXCEL-
LENT STORY TELLER, WITH AN
UNUSUAL SENSE OF HUMOR
WHICH MANY PEOPLE ARE SUR-
PRISED TO FIND IN INDIANS.

MORNING STAR — BETTER KNOWN
AS AGNES CLARKE. SHE IS
A DESCENDANT OF ONE OF THE
PROMINENT FIGURES OF THE
FUR-TRADING DAYS WHO MAR-
RIED A BLACKFEET WOMAN. A
GIRL OF GRACE, BEAUTY AND
EDUCATION, SHE IS ACTIVELY
ENGAGED IN THE MODERN BUSI-
NESS LIFE OF THE RESERVATION.

SHORT MAN — ANOTHER CHAR-
ACTERIZATION OF THE PICTUR-
ESQUE PECUNNIE INDIAN SIGN-
LANGUAGE EXPERT. HE IS ALSO
KNOWN AMONG HIS OWN TRIBES-
MEN AS BIG LEFT ARM.

NIGHT SHOOTS — A MEMBER OF THE PECUNNIE BRAVE SOCIETY. AN OUTSTANDING DANCER AND A PICTURESQUE FIGURE AT ALL THE BLACKFEET MIDSUMMER FESTIVALS.

SCALPING WOMAN — WIFE OF NIGHT SHOOTS. THE BACKGROUND IS TYPICAL OF TEPEE LININGS WHICH ARE DESIGNED BY THE WOMEN OF THE PLAINS TRIBES.

BUFFALO BODY — WEARING A
CEREMONIAL BUFFALO HORN
HEAD-DRESS. THOUGH SMALL
IN STATURE, HE WAS A GREAT
WARRIOR, HAVING MANY TIMES
SUCCESSFULLY RAIDED GROS
VENTRE AND SIOUX CAMPS,
CAPTURING MANY FINE HORSES.

JIM BLOOD — AN OLD PECUNNIE BRAVE, NOW FEEBLE AND AL-MOST BLIND. AS A YOUNG MAN HE LIVED WITH THE CROW IN-DIANS FOR FIVE YEARS. AFTER HIS RETURN TO HIS OWN PEOPLE HE LED A NUMBER OF RAIDS AGAINST HIS CROW FRIENDS, ALWAYS RETURNING WITH MANY FINE HORSES.

LAZY BOY — BLACKFEET MEDI-
CINE MAN. THE BACKGROUND
SHOWS HIS WAR HISTORY. IN
HIS HANDS HE HOLDS THE EAGLE
WING MEDICINE FAN AND WHIP.

WALKING BEAR — A YOUNG FULL
BLOOD INDIAN BRAVE OF MAJES-
TIC APPEARANCE AND CARRIAGE.

NOT REAL BEAR WOMAN — PICK-
ING KINNIKINNICK. THE SMALL
LEAVES OF THE BEARBERRY
PLANT (HEATH FAMILY) ARE
DRIED IN THE SUN OR OVER AN
OPEN FIRE AND MIXED WITH
SMOKING TOBACCO. THEY GIVE
THE SMOKE A PUNGENT AND
NOT UNPLEASANT ODOR.

WHITE DOG — AN EXCELLENT STORY TELLER WHO KNOWS ALL THE OLD STORIES WHICH HAVE BEEN HANDED DOWN FROM GENERATION TO GENERATION.

TOUGH BREAD — AN OLD WAR-
RIOR AND MEDICINE MAN OF
THE BLOOD TRIBE.

MORNING BIRD — ONE OF THE YOUNGER BRAVES OF THE BLOOD TRIBE. HE IS WEARING AN ELK-SKIN SHIRT RICHLY EMBELLISH-ED WITH TYPICAL BLACKFEET DESIGNS IN PORCUPINE QUILLS AND BEAD WORK.

BIG FACE CHIEF — A STALWART
MEMBER OF THE NORTH PIEGAN
BAND OF BLACKFEET OF CANADA.
HIS NECKLACE AND EAGLE WING
FAN MARK HIM AS A MEDICINE
MAN. THE NECKLACE, A BE-
STOWAL UPON HIM AT THE SUN-
DANCE, IS EVIDENCE OF HIS HIGH
STANDING AS A HEALER WITH
HERBS AND INCANTATIONS.

STRIPED WOLF — A PROMINENT MEMBER OF THE BLOOD TRIBE. A LEADER WHO IS RECOGNIZED BY HIS PEOPLE AS A MAN OF EXCELLENT JUDGMENT. HE HAS A GREAT RECORD AS A HUNTER AND WARRIOR.

TURTLE AND HIS SON, SETTING
MOUNTAINS—TURTLE, A FAMOUS
BEAR HUNTER AND DANCER, HAS
BROUGHT UP HIS SON WITH THE
OLD TRADITIONS OF HIS RACE AS
A GUIDE, WITH THE RESULT
THAT SETTING MOUNTAINS IS
ONE OF THE FINEST YOUNG
DANCERS IN THE TRIBE.

LAZY BOY — THIS PORTRAIT OF
ONE OF THE MOST GENIAL AND
FUN-LOVING CHARACTERS OF THE
PECUNNIE TRIBE, SHOWS HIM IN
HIS EVERYDAY COSTUME.

PLUME — A MEDICINE MAN OF
THE BLOOD TRIBE. SUCCESSFUL
OPERATOR·OF A RANCH ON THE
BELLY RIVER IN SOUTHERN AL-
BERTA. PROUD OWNER OF MANY
LODGES, HORSES, AND A LARGE
HERD OF CATTLE. AS A YOUNG
MAN HE WAS KNOWN AS THE
MOST HANDSOME AMONG ALL
HIS FRIENDS.

Page 60

ARROW TOP — PECUNNIE BRAVE
SMOKING A RED STONE PIPE.
SUCH PIPES ARE MADE FROM
SOFT STONE AND ARE SOME-
TIMES EMBELLISHED WITH IN-
TERESTING CARVINGS.

FISH WOLF ROBE — ONE OF THE YOUNGER BRAVES OF THE PECUNNIES, A POLICE OFFICER ON THE RESERVATION, THE FATHER OF A LARGE FAMILY AND ONE OF THE OUTSTANDING BLACKFEET DANCERS.

SINGING IN THE CLOUDS — A
BLACKFEET CHILD WITH DOLL
WHOSE HAIR IS MADE FROM A
SCALP LOCK TAKEN IN AN IN-
DIAN WAR.

CLEARS UP — ONE OF THE MOST
PICTURESQUE FIGURES AT THE
CEREMONIES AND FESTIVALS OF
THE PECUNNIES. VERY CAREFUL
AND IMMACULATE IN HIS AP-
PEARANCE.

EAGLE HEAD — 108 YEAR OLD
BLACKFEET WARRIOR, WHO IN
HIS YOUTH HAD MANY AN EN-
COUNTER WITH THE CROW IN-
DIANS, HAVING TAKEN SEVERAL
SCALPS AND STOLEN MANY FINE
HORSES. HE ALSO BEARS THE
NAME STRONG, WHICH WAS CON-
FERRED UPON HIM BECAUSE OF
HIS ACTIVITY AS A WARRIOR.

WINOLD REISS

For a decade or more Winold Reiss has dedicated his talents to creating a pictorial epic of the North American Indian which shall preserve the distinctive characteristics of these fast vanishing tribes. The Indians of the Northwest have been his favorite subject for research and the large number of portraits and figure compositions in color and in line which he has made of the Blackfeet Indians constitutes a veritable saga of the tribe.

Mr. Reiss has brought to his task an unusual and paradoxical combination of talents . . . his interest in racial type and character and his unfailing eye for the decorative aspects of his subjects. Indianologists commend Mr. Reiss's studies of the aborigines for their ethnological accuracy and the knowledge of custom and folklore which they display; and those in search of decorative art which shall also have an authentic American note are very apt to commission Mr Reiss for the carrying out of their ideas.

It is perhaps another paradox that a painter of German birth should have been a pathfinder in discovering the decorative possibilities of the North American Indian. Mr. Reiss was born in the Black Forest and received his training as an artist with his father, Fritz Reiss, well known genre painter specializing in the peasant types of the Black Forest, and with Franz von Stuck at the Royal Academy in Munich.

In common with many other German boys whose imagination had been stirred by Fenimore Cooper's novels, Mr. Reiss had a romantic interest in the North American aborigines. He wanted above all else to paint them. But his romantic imaginings were tempered by an artistic training which demanded accurate observation of character. And so he decided to come to America in 1913 for the express purpose of studying the North American Indian in his native habitat and also to introduce modern decorative art, which, although a flourishing and accepted style in Munich and Vienna, where it had its origin, was practically unknown in the United States. The Crillon Restaurant, which Mr. Reiss decorated in 1920, was the first demonstration of the decorative possibilities of the new style. Since that time Mr. Reiss has been one of the outstanding pioneers in introducing a modern decor which should harmonize with American architecture and express American taste.

It is true, of course, that American artists had painted the American Indian before Mr. Reiss dedicated his talents to interpreting their racial characteristics and customs. But in the majority of cases the point of view had been either purely ethnological or sentimentally inaccurate. Mr. Reiss was the first painter who saw the Indian abstractly as subject for art, who recognized classic monumentality in the manner in which he folded his blanket about him and in the proud carriage of his head. His pictures have helped to restore and give reality to the legend of the noble redman and have made him an epic figure among the lost and vanishing races of mankind. He has been able to achieve this quality of universality without sacrificing his realistic approach. Mr. Reiss believes that the epic of the American Indian should be preserved in murals for future generations on the walls of our public buildings and schools.

Since 1933 Mr. Reiss has been assistant professor at the College of Fine Arts of New York University. He also conducts a summer school at Glacier National Park. His most recent decorations are mosaic murals designed for the Cincinnati Union Terminal Building, depicting the history of American railroad building and the extension of the frontier.

HELEN APPLETON READ.

FRANK BIRD LINDERMAN

Love of the wilderness was in the blood of Frank Bird Linderman. The first Linderman to land in America came in 1690. Lindermans pioneered in New York State, in Pennsylvania and Ohio. When as a boy, Frank Linderman reached the shores of Flathead Lake, fifty years ago, he was seeking not the "Wild West" of cow towns and mining camps, but the wilderness. There he learned Indian ways and lived as they did. To know them better he mastered the sign language—an accomplishment which caused him to be known among them as *Sign-talker*, sometimes *Great Sign-talker*.

The first Indian he ever talked to was Red-Horn, a renowned Flathead. Linderman's account of their meeting, the inception of a lifelong friendship, is moving and beautiful. The boy didn't know a Flathead from a Kootenai, nor whether Indians were friendly or hostile, and of course the sign language was Greek to him; but he recalled long afterward that Red-Horn had been at great pains to impress him with the fact that he was a Flathead, not a Kootenai—who were hostile—telling him this in sign language over and over.

"No greater tenderfoot ever entered the wilderness than I," Linderman says, "and I am sure none ever took to the life more surely or more happily." Indians have always been his friends, though he did have some trouble with the Kootenais in the eighties, and a breathless narrative the story of that trouble is.

Linderman's Blackfeet name is Iron-tooth. The Crows call him *Sign-talker*. The old Kootenais named him *Bird-singer* and the early Crees and Chippewas called him *Sings-like-a-bird*. His name is one to conjure with among the Crees and Chippewas. They call themselves Linderman Indians, because—wrung by their pitiable homelessness—he was instrumental in wresting from a dilatory and indifferent Government the Rocky Boy (Stone Child's) reservation near Havre, Montana.

Twenty years ago Linderman went back to the shores of Flathead Lake. At Goose Bay, where he had trapped with the Indians, he built a spacious lodge for his family. He now retired from business to devote his time to writing—that he might record the Indian way of life that had passed; a culture no white man could ever again have opportunity to observe. His INDIAN WHY STORIES, AMERICAN, RED MOTHER, MORNING LIGHT—twelve books carry that record. Linderman knows the plains Indian as few men have capacity for knowing him. He knows the Indian too well to assume that he, or any man, can wholly grasp the mystic and spiritual significance of Indian culture. He has a fury of scorn for the superficial and faked "knowledge" that distorts and misrepresents and cheapens the story.

His lodge reflects the varied interests of his life. There one finds Indian artifacts, never to be duplicated, gifts from the great of their tribes; mementoes of the time when by sheer determination to *know* he made himself assayer of the old Curlew mine, and ended as chief assayer and chemist for the Butte and Boston smelter; cartoons of his unprized political life, when he sat in the State Legislature, or served as Deputy and Acting Secretary of State; and his manuscripts which are his being. Above all, his home reflects the happiness of his domestic life, and the memory of enduring friendships. Daughters and grandchildren visit Mr. and Mrs. Linderman there.

But the Indians of his boyhood come no more. Their campfires are burning for him among the Sandhills.

GRACE STONE COATES.

INDEX

BLACKFEET PORTRAITS